I0168368

NIGHT SETTLES UPON THE CITY

Omar Sabbagh

Daraja Press

Published by
Daraja Press
https://darajapress.com
Wakefield, Quebec, Canada

© 2024 Omar Sabbagh

Cover design: Kate McDonnell

ISBN 978-1-998309-33-7

Library and Archives Canada Cataloguing in Publication

Title: Night settles upon the city / Omar Sabbagh.
Names: Sabbagh, Omar, author
Identifiers: Canadiana 20240494776 | ISBN 9781998309337 (softcover)
Subjects: LCGFT: Poetry.
Classification: LCC PR6119.A23 N54 2024 | DDC 821/.92—dc23

Omar Sabbagh has long brought us a world in which personal experience stitches a hyphen between the eastern Mediterranean and the northerly British archipelago. Now he makes the tension inherent within that richness explicit, in a love-letter to his family and home city of Beirut.

Written while the 'night' of war 'settles upon the city', his introductory 'Thoughts' show us how unthinkable war remains, even when it arrives on the doorstep. This is a book of witness to what cannot happen, and yet does.

> – **Fiona Sampson, MBE FRSL**, author of *Two-Way Mirror: the life of Elizabeth Barrett Browning* (Washington Post Book of the year, New York Times Editors' Choice, finalist Plutarch Prize, finalist PEN Jacqueline Bograd Award, Sunday Times paperback of the year)

The poet Omar Sabbagh lives in Beirut. His voice is playful, almost surreal at times. He talks of 'the hairbrained monocle of war' and suggests that if you live long enough in a place like Beirut 'laughter becomes a lover's distance-giving kiss'.

Night Settles Upon the City offers us a poetry that is neither ideological nor partisan, not of the frontline but of a deeply threatened warzone. Its terms are easy-going, sorrowful, humane, formally intelligent and tinged with apprehension. It is humanity being human. Reading it is relief and hope.

> – **George Szirtes, FRSL**, T.S. Eliot Prize winner

Night Settles Upon the City by Omar Sabbagh is a profoundly reflective and evocative collection that blends personal experience with the brutal realities of life in a war-torn Beirut. Through a tapestry of poems, essays, and prose, Sabbagh explores the intersections of love, grief, intellectual contemplation, and the relentless backdrop of violence. The writing oscillates between moments of tender introspection and stark depictions of societal collapse, embodying a kind of philosophical meditation on suffering and survival.

Sabbagh's voice is distinctively lyrical, capturing both the intimacy of individual loss and the broader existential weight of conflict. His reflections on war and its aftermath are imbued with a sense of historical consciousness, yet deeply grounded in the immediacy of personal anguish and resilience. The collection is not just about bearing witness to destruction, but also about finding fragments of humanity amidst the ruins. A haunting and powerful work that invites readers into the fragile space between beauty and despair.

> – **Dr. Pamela Chrabieh**, Kulturnest Co-founder & Managing Director

The Arabic term for poet means *the one who feels*, unlike the Greek origin of poetry which describes the craft itself. Omar Sabbagh is the quintessential poet in the Arabic sense. In this collection, he vibrates with Beirut, where he now lives, at a time when the city's famous cultural vibrations are overwhelmed by murderous quakes caused by the Israeli war machine.

> – **Gilbert Achcar**, Professor of Development Studies and
> International Relations at SOAS University of London

Omar Sabbagh is a poet who is privileged to write about war and destruction from the relative safety of his study. But this double-edged illusion is insidious — mental and emotional inwardly, and physical for those who are directly under attack. It is visceral, political, heart-wrenching — yet the poet seeks out light and hope through the act of writing, for the sake of ownership and sharing. He may say that "I cannot read minds and nor / will I ever wish to", but he writes for the importance of record-keeping, seeking solace, both private and public — as the Night Settles Upon The City of Beirut.

> — **Sudeep Sen**, Winner of the Rabindranath Tagore Literary Prize

Alongside unimaginable horror we are shown the ordinary griefs and losses that we all suffer – of ageing, of failing, of being human; and it's the humanity and compassion with which Sabbagh bears witness that will secure this book's future among the handful of classics that will come to define our era.

> — **Jenny Lewis**, MA Oxon., MPhil., PhD, Tutor for Poetry,
> Oxford University

For my father and mother,
Mohamad and Maha Sabbagh,
without regrets
and for **Alia,**
light of my life

About The Author

Omar Sabbagh is a very widely published poet, writer and critic. Over the last two decades, his poetry has appeared in many prestigious venues, such as: *Poetry Review, PN Review, Agenda, Acumen, New Humanist, (T&F) New Writing, The Reader Magazine, Stand, Kenyon Review, New England Review, Banipal, The Warwick Review, The Wolf Magazine, Poetry Wales,* among many others. He has published six poetry collections and one pamphlet with Cinnamon Press, including *My Only Ever Oedipal Complaint* (2010), *Morning Lit: Portals After Alia* (2022) and *For Echo* (2024).

His Beirut novella, *Via Negativa: A Parable of Exile,* was published with Liquorice Fish Books in March 2016; and his Dubai novella, *Minutes from the Miracle City,* was published with Fairlight Books in July 2019. He has published much short fiction, too, some of it prize-winning. A study of the œuvre of Professor Fiona Sampson, *Reading Fiona Sampson: A Study in Contemporary Poetry and Poetics,* was published with Anthem Press in 2020, and was released in revised, paperback edition at the end of 2021. His book of Lebanese verse narratives, *Cedar: Scenes from Lebanese Life,* was published with Northside House in summer of 2023; and a collection of his published short fictions, *Y Knots,* was published with Liquorice Fish Books in autumn of 2023.

He holds a BA in PPE from Oxford, three MAs, in English Literature, Creative and Life Writing, and Philosophy, all from the University of London, and a PhD in English Literature from KCL. From 2011-2013 he was Visiting Assistant Professor of English and Creative Writing at the American University of Beirut (AUB); and he taught at the American University in Dubai (AUD), where he was Associate Professor of English from 2014-2024. From Fall 2024 he begins a new teaching role at the Lebanese American University (LAU).

Contents

'She walks in beauty, like the night...'
Lord Byron

Thoughts Upon An Intellectual Luxury From A City Besieged

Beirut

There's this luxury of course. To be free to write, sat at my ease, in a (relatively-speaking) safe part of Beirut, while bombs lay siege to its more southern parts. Though I have some of the broad lineaments of the politics at play here to hand, I'm not in any way overly well-informed about the details, the nitty-gritty of the why or wherefore of this group or that, or of this sect or the other. That, too, is probably evidence of luxury. However, seated here in the dining room of my parents' rather large, grand, plush Beirut home, it occurs to me there might be some potential value in trying to tease-out some integrated thoughts about (and about) what's going on here. I'm off-work, after all. The university I recently joined here has, after governmental instruction, closed shop for the rest of this working week, gifting me another kind of luxury, some more free time. Indeed, freedom is I suppose what is most at issue here, in so far as I want to use this prosy space to think-through, errantly perhaps, a conundrum that I find pressing intellectually – even if me thinking these thoughts is not of urgent or dire practical impact. Who after all, am I? No one. Anyone. Everyone.

I'll start by mentioning an old notion aired often by Edward W. Said. Asked his views at different times I believe regarding this or that Middle-Eastern war, he was wont to speak in effect of the speciousness of a zero-sum mindset. For instance, regarding the first Iraq war, he averred that both sides were overtly in the wrong and that one really didn't have to choose sides: that fascism, tyranny on the one side and ravenous empire on the other meant that one needed to be and could be critical of both at the same time. That it wasn't a crusade-like matter of: 'you're either with us, or against us.' I imagine though, one immediate way of bickering with this kind of stance is to call it, as well, a kind of intellectual's 'luxury.' That most people in this world hadn't or haven't the time or freedom to judge like this, the very materiality of their existence depending on the outcome of whatever war or conflict it might be. And one might say the same thing about the Russia-Ukraine war. Arguments can be made on both sides, of course, about the relative weighting of the wrongs embodied by either side, but the question remains whether such free-floating intellectual stances are valid, or if they are

1

indeed an indication of luxury, obtuse to the stringencies and exigencies in and of the lives of most on this afflicted planet.

My political instincts, for instance, have always been very left of center. (I say instincts because my leftist views were and are the product of both intellectual principle but also of a temperamental compassionateness.) So: taking the example of the Russia-Ukraine war, and thinking against the grain of the main, western-based media outlets, it just is the case that, as with Israel and Palestine, or Israel and Lebanon today – that the wars afoot have preceding contexts often swept under the carpet. The Palestinians of course have been terrorized, oftentimes indiscriminately and without hope of redress, for close to a century. And NATO forces had, as I understand it, made some highly questionable and aggressive geopolitical moves, interloping significantly on Russian-interests, well before the war with Ukraine. But here lies the rub of the conundrum I want to try to finesse here: do I, a UK citizen, born and bred, a child and youth and adult who in so many flagrant ways benefitted from the boons of living in a civil democracy (if not really 'democratic' socio-economically), a youth and then adult who had all the advantages of freedom and the opportunities for flourishing that that freedom granted me – do I have the right to oppose western interests? Even 'intellectually?' Am I not, through nearly every existential fiber of my body, compromised: in so far as I really don't have a choice, in so far as the choice is already made for me? And I think the crux of it comes down to two basic ways of thinking of ourselves as situated social or political animals in this world. Of course, the attractions and argumentative weights of both ways of viewing ourselves are evident. However, I want to make some sort of decisive incision here, into what all this means. And to suggest in the end the fact that intellectual stances are not in some way islands of being is in part the point of these ruminations.

So, I'll jumpstart these reflections by returning to Edward W. Said. He was famed to have rejected the on the face of things more practicable solution to the fraught history of Israel/Palestine, of a 'two-state solution,' in favor of a single, all-inclusive state. Principle aside, and normative wishes aside, this so-called 'utopian' stance has from a different angle of vision or approach an equally practical aspect to it. After all, models in real, empirical history, from Roman civilization or, later, Ottoman rule, seem to suggest that this kind of multi-faceted but still unitive state or political entity not only works and worked, but was in comparison with the other 'reality,' of our present world, a far more practical, pragmatic or indeed prudential model; especially when we are responsible enough in our intellectual stances to think not in terms of today or tomorrow, but in terms of something far more lasting. Analogues to such stances, whether utopian or just far-sighted, have occurred to me over the years, as my ruminations have wandered. I'll give two examples here of such intellectual divagations, before ending by picking-up the central thread again.

The first thought-experiment, was to imagine that undergraduate degrees were no longer on the whole undertaken at the age of eighteen or nineteen or twenty, say, but rather from the age of thirty or thirty-one. Quite unlike the suddenly liberated licentiousness of late adolescence, young adulthood, where even interested students still want to spend a significant amount of time recreationally in one way or another, a man or woman at thirty or thereabouts would, I imagine, be far more readied to invest nearly all their energy in their courses, reading every suggested book, following each line of enquiry or study with assiduity. Of course, that's not how the world works and so this supposition may seem highly 'utopian;' but in the sense detailed above it is also from a more epic standpoint quite realistic or true to the way life is, developmentally, for the most of us.

My second thought-experiment was a bit more politicised. We all know, for example, that corruption is present in much of the world and is hard to excise because of the vicious cycles its practice involves and has involved. But think on this: imagine a notoriously corrupt African state. Imagine a sixty or sixty-five-year-old diplomat or politician who knows quite well, from experience and from political nous, that things won't improve in this respect, or in any tangible sense, for decades and decades to come – and that, only potentially. Imagine he's approached and coopted by western interests: he is more likely to enact corruption, given the fact that change in his own national vicinity – which he may well have sincerely wished-for – won't be facilitated until well after he's dead, and given, let's say, the need to put two of his children through an expensive university system in the US, to give them a good start in life. That is, in a manner of speaking, the way of the world. But then, imagine in fifty years' time, with much medical advancement, the average life-expectancy becomes one hundred and twenty or one hundred and thirty years of age, as distinct from, say, eighty. Suddenly, the kind of vicious cycle detailed above would be hollowed, potentially, vitiated, because now the good intentions of our subject would have a workable chance and corruption would seem less enticing or indeed inevitable. Yes, this last is indeed an optimistic and hopeful gambit in thought, but is, again, given the way medical science develops and has of late developed, not entirely unthinkable.

So, what, I think, it comes down to is the angle of vision one chooses. Being far-sighted need not be dubbed 'utopian' or wishy-washy. At the same time, each one of must also live in his or her present, aware of if not necessarily immediately affected by the exigencies of that present conjuncture, near or far or in between. Indeed, all this ponderousness of mine, after all, might feel like thinking as luxuriance – while Rome, as it were, burns. But then, thinking like this, in this mode, does not emerge from or is not engendered by happiness or complacent luxury. I think the very spur and trigger of thinking like this, a touch ambitiously, is itself rooted in the ruts of our daily, empirical existence. It is not from a safe position, necessarily, that one ventures to think outside the box: it could be argued that the horrors or sadnesses of our world drive us or challenge us to think big, just as much as they draw us into the empirical nitty-gritty of any extant state or situation.

Just so, I've just spent the last hour or so writing-out these thoughts. Beirut – a different part of Beirut, given – is under siege. In the immediate sense, I find myself in a very fortunate enclave in a very unfortunate eventuality or reality. But I would argue, in line with some of the above, that this luxuriance I make-use of, this comparative freedom and safety, is not wholly irrelevant to those being bombed and harried from their homes and their very existence. If we all of us only thought about our immediate vicinities, we would never wander far from home in our thoughts or actions, from selfishness in mind or body, so to speak. Perhaps a little distance-giving luxury is needed to try and see the world straight; a world that needs more than just needs, a world that might also meet some at least of our well-intentioned desires.

Prologue

Fluency

For Maha Faris Sabbagh, on her 80th birthday
Beirut

You tell me things for goodness
to land like a patient bird and a brace
to brace my ruffled feathers,
forbidding certain sorry bird-lines, certain lines
of flight, making order from out of the winglessness

of its opposite. I have been so lucky
in my lucklessness, each bough a perch,
each of your chiseling strokes seeing in a block of stone
the pattern sent to lend me flight, bare
rock become beauty, figure...

And how many times we die in this life!
How many stations to stop the mind, guide it to its better church.
It was the pit-stops, the living detail of your mother's love
that built structure through the gifts of me, my I, my fluent sea.

Madness Through The Heart Of Creation

For Elise Salem
After Plato's *Phaedrus*
Beirut

When steeped in the mauve and marrow-colored soil
of his spilling words, the way they seem to enjoy
themselves, like the twinning tails of doves;
when busy building things, the facts he tries to make from love
and care – *it's just then* that the genie in the bottle,
rubbed-gold giving-on-to a greener apparition,
the ghost that will grant you the diamond pen
of all your wishes – *it's just then*, the mind goes brittle,

losing its hold, like sunstroke on the savannah,
or being drenched, a thickset brother to foliage,
by monsoon rains that are close to mystic.
You will never understand his ardor, the vintage
distilled by time, the bouquet of the richer wine, tasted on the air,
when the rules of grammar start to play, blind-eyed and wise, limbs-alive,
    limber, plastic.

War Diary

Li Beirut

London

Acres of wisdom, but touched, dotted like a bad dream
made to sound and scream your final resonance –
a city once a pulse and beat beneath my feet,

a city that was never fit, hale, whole, never clean,
a city sullied by hopes trolled into troll-like stone –
eager eyes swept-away, aging all the zealous wishes

that were the *Once* of a once upon a time...
Old lady by the sea, coupled with a cynic's wit;
old man, caged beneath the middle of the sunshine

that belongs to others, always, relentlessly –
where do you go now for solving or for solace
when there's only so much space on a bleeding planet?

Your future seems to be set by dust, your dusk, your past:
never an agent with a will to choose her way,
never the chance even to opt for death, or for how you'll die.

The Great Writer & His Place In The World

or

Gate Of The Sun

Elias Khoury, RIP
Beirut

You will hear him mentioned, mouthed
at the dizzy corner of a busied street
in a city of dross and dust and dirt,

a man they speak-of with marble words,
phrases hewn from the whitest alabaster –
a facet, let us say, of that old and sacred sculpture
that stands-in for the world, a figure
of beauty by which the world stands.

And his place in the world might just be
a place that heats beneath
the world, where he stokes the coals
that make it turn and move and breathe
through lungs that can bear the rapture
of the future moving into place.

And he will move us – and this is the grandest
thing of all – even when he's moved-on, away,
his pages like pregnant umber soil
beneath the gifts of water and the gate of the sun –

and caging time caged in ways
it had never, in truth, counted on.

To The Ghost Of Edward W. Said

Dubai

Blood boils, spreading heat like a rumor
beneath the skin. Anger's no more roof of flesh here,
finding its rivulets diverted, led astray,
waters that gush their red, failing to find their way
into anything but rage, the unreliable narrator.

And while the buzzards complicate the sky,
and undue death proves so hard to take,
burdening the sanity in all of us, who aren't quite saints,
I imagine you, restless now in your resting place.

Your printed words are not the final matter here;
more a spirit we sense upon the killing air,
a questioning face quick to turn its face
to face us, rummaging through all the trash and lies,
asking in tremors its urgent questions – at a time
when sterling questions are seen as lepers
banished to a colony of the nearly-dead.

All can read the print today, the arcane horrors;
gory words that splash upon us like spurting blood;
and your books, read aloud or left unread, stay
dogeared witness, living paper, breathing ink
of one whose thoughts still seem to think.

I cannot throw a livid rock like you – I've never
earned that right. But I can watch its flightpath through the air
and listen still to the searing music made,
and hear its spirit, its soundness sounding against awful murder,
rushing in pulses that seem to light my ears
with drummed defiance; giving trouble to the same-old ruse
of those with far less spirit, the zero-sum game
as ever of those flimsy ghosts.

The Day After

After the remote attacks in Beirut, September 2024
Beirut

Our pockets are full of blood,
as we hoard what we cannot hoard,
and lives that might have taken flight
and soared, have flown-away now
to the bower of a very different God
to that nightly visitor the killers of the light
bow to, snuffing as they do the innocent and the dead.
We, the survivors, must now fill the hollows

left-over, and think again of the impossible:
what those who've passed might have wished
and done, the tattered paper of their bucket lists,
the small, shy children of their vanishing wills.
How does one speak to the victims of horror,
when all we have are lips and paltry words?

The Joyful Wisdom?

After the remote attacks in Beirut, September 2024
After Nietzsche
Beirut

The dying sage wishes us to become
like fluid aristocrats – after the wisdom he'd found
in some antique, long-gone Grecian home;
to take the slights and slurs of living, full-on –
pugilists, if you like, deafened to the pain
that strikes then reigns across us, dying endlessly.
The phrase *'it is what it is'* would have been
like a kind of clever tenderness for him.

But we can't but look-back and rue in this life.
We're driven to reflect as much as we are to love
and die, loving. And for all the bravery
of his philosophy, we must brave it and reply
that the skin of our deepest suffering must be dyed
by the utmost color of our being weak and human.

An Afflicted City

Beirut

Perhaps it's true that love
came from the hands of a carpenter, the trophy of the heart
sawdust on a sunny morning?

Perhaps each song that lives
in any true or telling way must find it hard
to grapple with the words that make it fleshed,
ring true? That sacrifice proves the first
word to stoke the coals of any human effort
of worth, heating our skins, not from the morning of the sun,
but from the paradox of the blood within?

In this place, chaos on repeat,
you just cannot handle loss: it's too prim and tidy and neat,
just one more garment in the drawer
folded-away, moving to the drum of the next day, the next day,
to the beat of use and misuse,
feet in a frenzy of feet
footing and following feet –

the music of a people's cleverness, cunning,
tuned to a station of static, as they listen
now to a few scraps of scrappy sound, so grey
and fuzzy, it's clear: that all the skills of their intelligence
practice them for nothing but for honing
the techniques of being
lit and moved by this hopeless parody of living.

Besieged

After more attacks in Beirut
Beirut

It is morning again, but they have killed
the morning. The book of life is blood-smattered
and death is all we read, words and phrases
becoming pages, horrid leaf without leave, dogeared.

Even the connoisseurs of doubt
find a certain sort of tragic surety here
and are maddened by it, becoming strangers to themselves –
the world about them, the world they're used to,
filled with the shrapnel of a blind man's hate, the grapeshot
that is half a minus number, half a square root...

But for them it's an old, a selfsame story: besieged,
a sinister knife at the throat, the unseen rage
of an enemy caught in the cage of its own brittleness –

a coward from a distance, winning by flame and fire alone,
a foreigner to the morning, a ghost behind the sun.

Letter From Beirut

Beirut

On the other side of these words
there is a reader: let him or her
shake with fury,
because the buried dead have stayed unburied,

because of the utter, brazen scandal
of these, our livid events, men and women
and white-eyed children
vanished at the hands of a remote control,

the high and loud techniques
of a whole bestiary of beasts –

as the science that was meant to free us,
to let us climb and rise, progress,
becomes the primal tool of our desertion
from the human bond, the beacon of descent.

And if you, dear reader, placed on the other side
of these few notes, find their verve and their decisions
hidden from you like errant strangers, dead
and dud, please if you would think again:

injustice hurts more than anything else
because the welt of its human betrayal
insults God himself;

so, walk with us a while
and think once more of Donne, think of the bell
tolling for each one of us,
wronging or double-wronged;

walk with us into the gap
of our sheer unknowing
and feel what it's like to be like us, strung-up
like puppets, driven by the gusts and strings
of such selfish, warring children.

While Rome Is Burning

Beirut

The streets begin to mouth their cur-like doubts again,
stone-like cynics after years of being failed, let-down
by those who wield the reins
that might have made an ordered sailing
from this sad, sinister, sea-like formlessness –
that might have drowned the swallowing of the sea herself
and made of it a land upon which to land.

But home remains a foreign notion here.
The racking bombs are like pieces of the furniture
decking a home for a mind that's shared then tossed
upon the waves and waves of all things lost
and the bitter salt of *nothing doing, nothing doing.*
We drink fire here. Water is from a different life
it would have been nice, I think, to live.

Worldly Shadow

Beirut

The sunlight thrusts-out its batch of electric hearts,
sprites of the morning, wheeling, caterwauling
down in angles that cut across buildings, still standing.

We live in the city's safer, freer parts, but our thoughts
can't but move like traipsing children, held and burdened
by ward-like loads, can't but roam, rove, racked,

towards the city's south, where martyrs die
in smelted gold, where martyrs rise
in worldly shadows, shades above the tar-black flames, and tar-black

footage overtakes our minds and soot
becomes the working language, forked as forking, at hand –
the common food, the shared issue.

And soon, of course, it will be dark again, another day passed,
and the limbs of our reaching hearts will be cripples, shadowed, overcast.

Soullessness Afoot

In light of more attacks
Beirut

Down by Beirut's *Corniche* the other day,
down by the mint-green sea,
I watched the waves as though they were watching me –

each line of cloth-white froth,
each small bit of frittering spray
speaking for a place like this, this city
gutted now for gutted centuries,

racked and screwed beneath a wrecking light
like the creature it is,
but rutted the more by the fangs of a more savage beast.

There's so little that's truly wise
about the human animal,
as he bares his teeth then bites,
selfishly, ravenously,
so that all those parts that hid his soul –

beveling it or burying it
away from licit sight –

fall-away now, leaving only the body as a body of night;
a body made deaf to the song of its sometime, living birthright.

Night Settles Upon The City

Beirut

Night settles upon the city,
a panther's pelt slowly curving round us,
rich and blue and voluptuous,
enveloping us like memory

of the things we couldn't abide
and of the things we could.
Purple mixed with a thickset umber,
the night-sky's a hand filled with soil

that might've made so much,
flower after treasured flower,
but which now can only fail
to start what might have been, such

bounteous hopes, such childhood.
The world has a rich man's seal
embossed upon it, blood-red wax
stamped upon the unopened letter

whose words spell-out the detail
of dreams now-snuffed, desires
quashed beneath the attack
of this dark and violent animal.

In Other News

Beirut

It's been a lifetime like this,
our eyes riveted, glued to the TV.

To live in Beirut is a privilege
as long as you don't watch the news,
the old-new news,
the words that spill and tarry, only to unmake you
and to take from you
all that makes you glad here, free.

And so, we age here. We age
because what we watch, torn by doubts, daily,
is more relevant to us than water,
proving nothing but that we are the sons and daughters
of blind and violent mischief. And, in other news,

the poor and the afflicted have nothing more to lose.

War Diary

Beirut

Words on paper, tall green blades
swaying on a prairie, billowed by
a heartening wind; spilled language, a great lake
calming a thickset mind, quieting the eye
that looks upon it, steadier and steadier for it.
These are the images that gift me rest,

if not repose. We are resigned here
to face a faceless enemy, gripped and braced
by a faceless fear. But then,
they tell me that words
placed upon a paper might just solve the absurd
price that's paid each day here, a little bit,
a little bit, anyway...

Dear Diary,
listen to the bleeding of the artless art,
log and gauge the terrors of our times,
be a refuge for the homeless.
Be a place made sure by shoring pillows,
because history is here, right here – *yes, no* –
the vicious *quid pro quos.*

A Bookish Man Bereft Of Words

Beirut

When will the guns tear-up, well-up
with a lump in their throats?
When will arms be used for embracing another –
not to craze him, lose him, raze him? When will lips
be used between each other, as distant lovers
born of the same deeps, the same human tribe?
And when will words be used to dote
again, lettered like kisses from a mother to her son?
When will war, the untimely, be unbegun?

The truth is, no one really knows anymore:
not even God, I don't think, not even my father.
Our world seems to slip its skin – a misnomer
to itself. It's like a word hidden on a shelf
I cannot find, searching as I am through the bookstacks of hell.

Noises Of War

Beirut

Sirens wail their way across the streets below,
and once again, the distance between life
and death intoxicates the air.
And we are like tumbling drunkards here,

clasping our loved ones close, the furrows
that line the land of what means most to us,
the soil from which we grow, deeply, richly sewn –
but even that is not enough.

I was born, you see, in a land far more blessed;
freedom went ratcheted through all my bones,
and death was never there to make me feel I was all alone:

but these noises now that pollute the air about me,
these strangers in the dark – they seem to watch me, to see
through me, like questions that have no reply.

CNN Etc.

For Mohamad Sabbagh
Beirut

The old man buries his head in his hands.
His eyes, downcast, lowered. The inside of his palms
are secret maps he seems to be questioning.

His jowls have grown looser and flabbier of late.
His heart has aged. *This is Beirut*, he seems to say –
a place for an old man to get heavier and older.

Though the TV still blares its rot, he doesn't seem
to be listening anymore: as the day's end dies
as we've come to expect, bombs, the night's fluting.

The newsperson waxes on: but what's to understand?
That murder can be finessed, that violence and hate
can find themselves told in a smoothening, softening tale?

The old man shivers with the cold. The collateral
damage grows on the screen – these are the fallen petals
from the sun-sprung flowers of what might have been.

He looks up now, with tears in both his eyes:
this is Lebanon, he whispers, *the land of my fathers*.

A Tasteless Boast

Beirut

War is getting worse here, deepening its hold.
Lebanon feels like the shrapnel of the world –
shards of weapons shattering the glass
of our insides. And our eyes are of course
made of glass here, touchable, vulnerable,
naked before the daylight, all questions asked
of us without reply. Each day might be a last.

War feels like a limb turned of a sudden limbless,
and yet still, not quite there, stitched-together, cast
with splints forged from the very air.
We wake and talk and eat like ghosts here,
wraiths passing between the erstwhile shadows
of the living. In short, we are not ourselves:
another day beneath the rasp of a razing evil,
another day in hell. And life feels like bragging. A tasteless boast.

Interlude:

Family Matters
and More Familiar Griefs

RIP John Burnside

Dubai

There was something so sweetly undecided
in the writing beneath the writing
and you knew the names of different trees
and your specialism seemed to be a specialty
in falling the fall of that falling wound we like to call *freedom*,
and ground-zero was a place you found
so far from home you made it spell and read
like a second one, better one. You'd the blood-soaked song
of the adventurer thrumming in your bones,
but so little violence to mark you with disgrace.
And in knowing, as you did, the different names
of different trees, as one who knows his dream
while dreaming, you found it easy to light the space
of all your nascent pages with better words than *time*,
the things that pass us by, coursing with their passing.
You've earned your slot of peace now, your bird-line
through the sky; and as we now turn-to it, attend, amazed, and listen,
it's the tenderness we hear, one who knew the hurt beneath the words.

Searching The Horizon

On landing a new job
Dubai

I opened my eyes and my eyes opened
the light that helped them first to arise;
and it was as though a window had forged another window,
working and sculpting the light to show
the drama of seeing sight – how a new horizon
glanced at me, gently, knighting me with angles,
the emanations in a cool and slaking breeze,
and the unmastered day ahead, like a slave still
to each of hope's refractions, each ghost
on its way to becoming the fuller filled-out flesh
it wants to be. Lit now, gripped by delight,
I walk among the staple daily shadows
and feel each one sundered below my stepping feet,
the horizon busied now with its batch of unhurt children.

The Ghost

Dubai

In the corner of the room
a cheap white frame; the picture inside
shows an aged man, minted there
with a brimming sense of achievement, calmed
by a certain slow and quiet pride.
My daughter kisses the picture
now and then, scurrying to that small corner
whenever trouble threatens.

The man there has seen it all before,
how each one of us holds his own white sky,
letting it fold upwards into each one of his own dark eyes;
how each one of us elides the fateful missive sent
him, an opened secret from above or below;
how each one of us living speaks
in stillness to himself as though he were a ghost
already, a spirit seeking to prick the fabric
of the world he's left behind,
hoping to needle the place it was that long ago
he'd signed with departure.

And between the two,
this framed wiseacre and my daughter,
I see my life past each day's silent slaughter
turn in style between white and grey,
framed by the two known sides of love.

Proving Weber Wrong
A Tribute to Waddah Faris, RIP

Waddah Faris, my maternal uncle, was livelier and larger in liveliness than the standard of any staple life. To say that he possessed and evinced charisma would be to exercise a euphemism. He lit and struck the places he inhabited with burning golden light. You'd walk into a room where he was, and his arms became wide-spanned wings of welcoming, his voice – deep and echoic and dramatic, as though emerging from some grotto or marrow-colored cavern – greeting you in a way that made you feel like you'd just made a million. He was if you like a connoisseur and a practitioner of the preemptive strike. You were bowled-over by the magic before you'd a chance to get a word in. Rapture, passion and enchantment were the keynotes of his being, and it was infectious. And what struck me most about this highly intelligent man, was that for all his encyclopedic knowledge of the fine arts, and for all his famed presence in the middle-eastern art-world, specifically – known and loved by anyone who was anyone in that world for over half a century – what he made indelible was his capacity for insight. It wasn't what he knew and its extent, it was, as with all kinds of wisdom, the way he could crack the shell, husk, and grasp the kernel – the chemistry of his knowledge and experience, rendered into quicks, alchemy. He made and developed winnings from each day of his life, I imagine. At ease in any company, worldly by any touring standard, he was though of a nomadic temperament. He spent the contents of his mind and his heart, never hoarding them like an anchorite. It was a quality I admired, because it was a facet of his character that I'd have loved to be able to emulate, chiseled as I am from a more obdurate stone; and he was unique in my experience in so far as he blended past any mechanical amalgamation the won sagacity of a contemplative with the hurried brio and stamp of a man of action. I think that was his secret: he dramatized, unfailingly, the results of his senses, always making the deeps of his highly-sensitized experience something to be shared, communed. In this sense he was religious: while not a practicing advocate of any official religion, this deeply-earthed man was just rigged to connect and re-connect with others, and with such warmed relentlessness that it's not at all surprising, these weeks after his passing, to see and read the glowing and glamorous tributes, an influx of sheer gratitude for the life he led and for the life he shared with others. He possessed, if anyone ever truly has possessed: well, real presence.

Watching My Father Grieve

For Mohamad Sabbagh
London

When someone you've known
your whole life dies
and wickerwork becomes the fabric
of your aching mind

and you must live in the hiatus
and become the flesh of your newfound sadness,
getting older and older, living the mistake
of extant fading being – I can understand
the feeling of abyssal loss
and of a hole finding its erstwhile home.

But when it's the son of someone you've known
your whole life's beating
who dies,
it's like a window falling out of your eyes.

Care

Beirut

What's it like, he says to himself,
For half your life to be carried by voices
You'll never know? The random cry
Of the outsider peering upwards, inwards,
The sly fault-line between you and them
That buckles, baulks, offering wavering dream
In place of the sturdiness of wokeness.
What's it like to be made of ending words,
Given your sentence in a line of eyes
That seem to grip you back against a wall,
That flatten what you think to what they do,
As though you were one of them?
What's it like to live in your self-styled sky,
But like a cloud whose whiteness is forfeit,
A cloud unseen for being just as blue
As the rounding air that circles it, anchors it,
And you, lost to sight? You were never there,
The vapid gusts seem to say, rising upwards
To rattle and shake the depths of the inner window
Of the self you know. You were us all along.
You, whom love had finished; you, who tried and dared
To be closed-off in closeness by the cloth of care,
Singing of your white forever – of white where white was wrong.

5

For Alia on her birthday

Imagine a world without number:
what would it look like? The air
we breathe would be so much simpler
to breathe. Worry and angst would leave their
shoes at the door of being, politer
for being closer to north
and we'd be the better able to feed ourselves
on life, peeling its rind for its flesh to tell
the darling of its fruit. But today it is number
of a different sort that counts: number without weight,
number bereft its entourage of saddened thoughts,
number as if by magic made into flowing water.
So, drink it up, my love, gulp and gulp and swill:
the swelling of life is ever yours to fill
with number, today of all days.
Be what you are meant to be and be
in the world of number, but without its tax or fee.

Image

London

Outside the window, morning clouds.
They seem to cling to the sky with love,
morning and coffee, bread, olives,
forgiven their trespass like the queuing dead
who crowd our memories, the pictures we have

of better mornings. And as their woken images
traffic the mind, they look to me like saints and waylaid sages
bodying the lighter road of a lighter, different life.

The red-draped voices beyond the window grope
and grapple, reaching to achieve a certain anger
in me, wishing a spur of fire to light these tapping lips.

But I've no time to wait for *No* or for forever:
the glue of the morning clouds adheres, a proof to me
of my finest figure – and I, a mirror of what I see.

The Wind Rustling Through The Window

London

The air is made of fallen leaves,
its rustling sound and rustling feel
say so. Lying back, letting it flow through
the precious key of the open window
I recollect now a different flat
in a different country, years ago,

if not decades back. It, too,
seemed to write the same kind and flawless lines
of poetry across bedded skin,
as though moving air could never end
what its sweetened noughts could only ever begin.

She is dead now, my grandmother,
but the mystery of time is not.
Between then and now and now
and then, the ghost of the juxtaposition
that keeps most of us afloat –

pairing two glad moments
of indolence, twinning the forts of two torn boats

of innocence – as it rocks upon the cares
of the same-old sea of time, a shadow
across coursing, tossing waves,

the same rudder, though, the same,
the same rigged sailing built into a name.

Editing Work

For Mohamad Sabbagh
London

The old and aging man
splayed upon the sofa, dragged by time,
visits the ears of those who'll listen
to his smallish pound of aching wisdom.

He speaks of the worst feeling
a man can bear, the worst, most losing sense
to snipe at him, working as it does to strip him
bare: *regret* – with its school of hollows, its stigmata
planted in a palm, saying *nothing doing, nothing...*

It's the feeling, he says, of the echo that cannot be
silenced, his lucid quiet now lost forever or for
the fort, slowly-sieged, of his remaining years...

But none of us, not even loving sons,
can feel the brimming emptiness that others feel
at times like these.

All we can do is to edit the poems
of those we love, shadowing their lifelong reel
with the ghosts of later falling words. Subtitles.

His New Office

LAU, Beirut

The emptiness bears a flavor at sunset.
There is so much to do and place.
So much to fix, to build, to make,

as I walk through the music
of different terrains – such notes
of uncanniness,
newness and emptiness,
the different plains on a new and windswept face.

And may the dream of prairies and lakes
walk with me, not into battle
but through the gift of a new-built grammar
of peacefulness
and grace – a friend to each call

to friendship. Soon,
the find of this vacant space will loose
itself into a fit of order:

live like a paradox, and feel like one
too. And I must try to go farther
and further than I have ever done.

Acrimony

Beirut

I watch her, searching the stone-jagged distance
between us; and it feels so much like a troubled dance,
two pairs of eyes, split and riven from each other

like the different backlogs that gird their colors:
where olive meets chestnut, or tan, or almond, and
sour fruit, prideful, serious, a wind-tickled skin.

We have been sparring, vying with each other,
each naming each an innocent in the realm of the innocence
of the other – when two bodies are robed in guilt

here, the gilded kind you'll never quite raze or spill
from the cup that brims with it. I ask her now to
detail and color the lived-in list behind her brows,

but she can only tell me what I already know:
that a seed must end its life in a flower of a different kind.

The Psychopath

For Dr George Resek
Beirut

They say he must be heartless,
seeing things come to pass
made to shatter the eyes
of eagles. They say

he was built by a kind of cleverness
that had no sibling, no loving breath
to be shared, no common-held truth
to shake the air in a communion of two or more.
They say many things to shut the door

of each moment, to stifle him
and silence him – as he lugs the batch of humming sins
he must carry up the cold-browed, sharp-edged mountain
that was made for him

by a mind that never belonged here.

And in the end, it was seen
the wide eyes of his genius, hidden to be found,
were placed in the slots of what he didn't do

and not in what he did. He's been blown
hither and thither for a thousand aging years
like an amber dot of pollen a flower
was once so proud to know.

Four Quarters Of A Seamless Sea

For Maha Faris Sabbagh, on her 80th birthday
Beirut

I awake this morning to a quiet house.
None stir. The sky on the other side
of the window is darkened and stilled,
and each time I place a word here,
moving stored mountains of sense
into play, from the inside of me to my outside,
I can feel the way you forge each sentence

from within me, the rhythm of your will
driven and driving from so long ago, serving to rouse
these gladly trusted friends upon my shoulder,
these braver angels, these finishers of fear.
One year on, and we find you a mother
of the tides that rock and sway
your children, four quarters of a seamless sea.

In The Era Of False News

For Alia
Beirut

The archives of the future will sting the mind
and there will be no more beehives
for retreat from the siege
of stinging. My daughter is

fascinated by bees and what they can do
when riled or threatened, but tells me I'm not
to worry, because her kisses stay forever,
protecting my skin, my flesh, her lips
like rind to circle my erstwhile soul.

And yet, I still worry for the young today,
and how they'll treat the acid quid pro quos
between now and then, at a time when the clock
will have descended, submerged
to the gluey-black of the black river,
one more victim to be drowned in the Styx –
no one left to know what that is.

The angels, though, live in their eons,
and my daughter knows what she's talking about:
the expertise she has about being is

something I treasure.

Poetry Makes Nothing Happen

Poetry Makes Nothing Happen

Beirut

I walk through this apartment
in West Beirut. It's a wide and graceful space
and the very air feels like it's lined with lace.
It's a privilege, after all, to be, or to feel, safe.
The whole night through the aggressor
has bombed, picking and culling-at life, dear life –
as though it weren't the unsung riddle that it is,
as though it were a pat and simple thing. Descent
becomes the new arousal here, as we wake
and keen and mourn the violent passing of those
we never knew, those we were never meant
to meet, those more unfortunate, weaker, poorer –
lives that were just as much like brimming mints
of riches as ours are. Poetry makes nothing happen
of course: except to hold a frail and shivering light
above the white blanket of a page, fighting the fight
with wordy weapons – used to unveil the blanketing night
that others, elsewhere, have no more words for.

Advice Once More For Horatio

Beirut

Think on the paradox of time: the past is
no more, I fear, the future, yet to be, the present
eliding capture – even by the chasing feet a poet
sets in-play, so prim and tidy and neat.

But for some, the paradox at-hand is so much more,
and the tension by which a tale is told, the spur
and trigger that may just take us – outcasts
that we are – from *A to B*, is not quite so heaven-sent.

And all the moves and tropes of your philosophy,
dear boy, will never serve the flesh we try to place
and fix on time, because there are others here, there are others,
and for them time's question's laced – past each and every cleverness –

with fear, vivid and relentless, slow and unsurpassable.
So, tomorrow will be the other's day again, the null-
point of being, and we will remain like strangers to each other
here – each and every one of us, caged or castled in his reality.

Monologue In The Voice Of Netanyahu

Beirut

Never again, never again, never, never.
I walk in beauty, like the elder son I am.
I tell my people they are not to worry
because the thing of it is: I am.

I tread upon the lives of others,
squash the bleeding life from them,
but I, and those I love, are the only lambs
to hand. I walk in beauty, never sorry

for the things I do, the things I've done; for
the crimes like strident peacocks that seem to come
from within me – my whip upon the backs
of those beneath my devilment, my dominion.

I walk in beauty. And each murderous attack
I order seems to drain this world of innocence.

All Bets Off Says The Pundit

For Mohamad Sabbagh
Beirut

The enemy, he says,
has always calculated.
The wickerwork of loss and gain
was always a pattern of figures for them
in a chain of reasoning
a man might come to comprehend.

But now, I fear, all bets are off.

There is a new sense of uncertainty
now, sheer will in a chancy wind;
a kind of radical perversity
that will bring us blinded-ness and bring
us nothing, nothing but trough
after trough, devolving, in a world
whose peaks are gone, frittered, their gems
of gemmy snow, white and fresh and cold
to the touch, sluiced-away, melted.

In the past one could look to the heights
in a time of lows. You might gauge the one
by way of the other, like twins who loved each other.

But now, I fear, it's naught
but thoroughgoing night
without let-up, and we are like lambs
to the proverbial slaughter,
the cogs of our minds jinxed
and stopped. The sunshine
of what's left of understanding shines
upon stranded bits and pieces; nothing links;
to connect two drops of water
into one
is now our simple failure.

The meaning of events
makes us thirsty, but our mouths just cannot drink.

Another Morning At The Front

Beirut

Below, the streets are quiet, close to empty.
The hooting traffic of Beirut's yesterday
feels like a mouse today, scurried into a hole.
We are the children here of what we've yet to know.
And even if the sun has risen, conquering
the chance of a more capricious, fickler God,
and even if two mountains or two hills
that touch at the bottom may just still
make a valley, and two plus two equals
four, still, a new tremor of unhomeliness is afoot.
Where do we land and park our bodies, call-out
in a shrill voice to some keep or home, when the dying
and dead cram each small space inside our throbbing heads?
Where is the place of the morning? Where might our hearts be fed?

Ritual

Beirut

The liturgy went sent back-and-forth
in Arabic, and yet I followed the priest's words,
speaking as he was of neighborly love, the mercy
of God. Of the image He's sewn like a failsafe eye
within each one of us, guiding us, as we dye
the world about us, how we color it with worth –
the white-skinned dignity that might just be our curse
while the human figure precedes the hearse
that will take him in the end. *Today of all days* –
a whole nation forced to revisit the blows of her relentless yesterday –
it was good to mourn in an Orthodox church.
The censer swung, releasing the fragrant smoke
that seemed to be freer than each one of us, sat or standing there –
each one of us, the victim of a cruel and fickle joke:
living in this benighted city, beneath the hairbrained monocle of war.

War Crimes

Beirut

Each time we hear a loud and noxious noise
from the cushioned safety of home
and think of disaster, an edict without reply,
living in our bodies here, like parasites upon our bones,

we are reminded of the crimes that brought us here,
to this place, this dust-ridden manger of anxiety, fear,
and how there just is no trite, miraculous birth –
at least not now, on this pat version of the spinning earth.

Let he who would accost a neighbor to defy
the decencies of any human inheritance, of the civilized,
the kindness between newfound strangers
that is the summary of all we've ever learnt

from the non-stop violence of history, the beasts
of that bestiary – let him now feast his eyes
upon these flaming, burning words, *and let him be burnt!*
Bread's born of flour; there is no happiness without peace.

Distant Sounds

Beirut

The ground beneath our feet tremors
now and then: we wish for earthquakes
and for the sigh at a more natural evil.

I awake to a morning ready to wake
again, and it feels once more like the enemy's far
from the rules that tide the animal kingdom,
that he is, not only a breaker of all or any human laws,
but like a raving, rabid beast,
frothing at the mouth, spilling his spit, his spittle,
ready to bite and infect the rest of us
with the sickness of his own wild and crazed disease:

hate, blind hate, and hapless violence in its train;
hate, like a league of locusts released across the vibrant plain
of the living, each one of us a tall and proud blade of grass,
each one of us a breath in the sway of a common wind.

And even though night – its dark, prolific murder – is far away,
one almost wishes for it, merely to finger the hope of another day.

Dahieh, Beirut, Lebanon

Beirut

This is an exercise of the imagination,
a pugilist I've trained to fight to his best.
I want him to spar in ways that might impress
the world that dithers about us; to loan
his grueling muscle to a cause that's blessed
by the rote-lined heart of anyone, anyone possessed

of a human imagination, any man, woman, fit
and ready and able to connect the elusive dots,
anyone with a moving vision that might just reach
farther than the small, shy self that groans – rich
with needlessness, or else, with an urgent need.

I want, in short, to feed the remnants of a god
and see life, harrowed as it is, from the other side;
to try at least to rise-above all of this, which stays a mere exercise of style.

The Parable Of The Old Men Laughing

For Mohamad Sabbagh and the card players
Beirut

I envy the old men their laughter,
their doubting humor, their composure.
Live long enough in a place like this
and laughter becomes a lover's distance-giving kiss,
a thing to release the self at-hand – with all of its
backlog of burdens, duties, all the humdrum shit it's
so used to carrying – from the strain, the stress;

to un-leaven once more the bread that rises
like an unwanted meal, to unmake the untimely provender –
their laughing, a smithy, if you like, to build survival,
to forge one more breath that works in the midst of all this mess.
I envy them their brio, the wild vitality of the old;
it's their way, I guess, of staying relevant, radical –
and to elide the steady wives of doing what they're told!

Mr. Kurtz Reconsiders: A Fiction

Beirut

There is a certain peace here, though the city burns.
It's not that the gifts of human care nor the fair
concern for others, spilling into death,
is lacking in him: it's just that he's reached a stage
in life in which the various outposts of theatre
have lost the pull they might once have had.

He now hails, it seems, from a different country
and the locals blister, boil, with no more rage
against his staying here. And his heart is far
from a heart of darkness. And its only enemies are
the brutish, drone-like soldiers who may just choose return
to colonize this land, this home, this burial ground.

But the enemy, he says, are bluster, and vacant breath;
they stride with arrogance, effrontery, to the sounds
of their war-like drums, but we'll refuse to play along.
What's more: as was said so well by one just passed
in a crashing swelter of choking martyrdom
let them come: the stunts of evil to stretch their longish arm.

Beneath the woken god of human solidarity,
beneath the swelling of a new-built Arab tide
what they bring cannot live, and will not last –
each one of us a note that joins and links, seamlessly,
in the patterned freedom of a human song;
each life, threading to its other, each life, and one life at a time.

Morning Coffee

Beirut

It's the routine, I think, the way the broken leg
of morning casts itself for the long haul
of recovery, that might just keep me sane.

But to predict betterment or remission may well be
to spar and tarry with a nameless future, possessed
of only one duly working eye – dragged
as it is into the work of two. Already, I miss
the sense of a white page, clean-run like a beggar, empty,
the white that welcomes the riches of the pen
like an honored guest, its freedom to draft and spell
the lines of its desires, freewheeling and just,
and never quite finished, and never quite drained.

My morning coffee stands in salute beside me
like a sentinel, but one that guards a slighter, lesser portal –
a gate, not to guide me away, but for me to enter the same-old world.

The Nightmare

For Mohamad Sabbagh
Beirut

I dreamt only the other day
of a slightly personal catastrophe.
In the dream I found myself beset
by a cancer of the lungs.

It was the day after my father's visit
to the hospital for this or that,
climbing the same-old rung-less ladder, but
duly girded by his son. Hand-in-hand we went
in this newborn country of return,
in a gambit for repayment of the debt
accrued like clots across the burning years:

he's been watching-over me, guarding
me, a private angel for so darned long,
it's about time I gave myself the eon,
too, that is the angelic mission of a son.

And so, who cares about the dream,
live and livid and living as it was: the waking present is and stays
a stirring sleepless sickness, fit
to wake us each and every day, burning with concern,

as foreign armies and impostors
traipse across this sovereign land, bearing troupes of worser things,
hairbrained charlatans that they are.

They make of each and every night
a time for fools. A far more faultless nightmare.

Crime And Punishment

Beirut

As a youth, it was these kinds of sorry tales
I warmed to. My soul, it seemed, was up for sale.
And to this day, I don't quite know
the full psychology of what comes below:

but it seems to me that I was rigged
to always feel the victim, and that even though
the truth was I'd done nothing really wrong, naught to jig
the punishment wending-in with welcome –

and felt it, too, proper, special, due, a way
for me to feel mildly heaven-sent, wailing well in martyrdom –
the cogs that wheeled and drove inside of me
were parts of my freedom still, if quick to cage and sell me.

I read Kafka, too, of course. The Lebanon of the day
merits no more hurt or suffering; and yet, through the crimes
she never added to the world, she's made in all her whiteness to feel a stray
once again. The flower of any likely rhyme here is like a broken stem.

Crowding *Hamra*

Beirut

They're not all draped in black,
crowding the streets of *Hamra*,
the body of the south, gutted now
and spilling down,
only to give to homelessness
a newly-reeking sound

beyond the bombing raids, and peeling
at the skin of those far better off
heat and brouhaha, the milling
of a people rutted, lost.

Streets were never made for this:
and perhaps it was in truth a garden lane
that was the word that most would lip
before the dark and screw-brained
drivenness of wild and fey attack?

It's not the dust-ridden-ness
holding in the grip
the grasp-less-ness of a well-trained
eye, it's something smaller, better
crossed by the same-old Arab weather –

it's the litter of real and beating human life.

Mathematics

Beirut

This land has always been a tool,
something to be used from a distance,
the playground of the warriors.

Larger forces that do not dare
to show their faces – the only honest, godly space
upon a needy body – traipse and tread and rule
in shameless secrecy, hiding their names
behind the front line of this warzone of innocents.
In fact, it has always been the same –

Lebanon bartered, sold, tossed like a wager raised
in the poker game of the bigger nations.

All her life, she's been forced and driven, driven to react,
and need has been the vein of it, not
the artery of desire –
never an agent for herself, never lit by her own dear light.

It's here, on the ground of this small and helpless land
of martyrs, that war makes its curse, its confession –
the pain of subtraction, its first, its only mathematics.

The Old Man And His Walking Stick

For Mohamad Sabbagh
Beirut

It gets worse each day, watching him
aging, the drain that seems to drag-at his limbs,
spindly and white and slowly thinning;
watching the old man as he begins to return
to his beginnings, a predictable route.

I idolize the wiseacre, a newborn son
each dawn, rising each day to start to pay the debt
I'll still be owing when *I'm* an old man –
if that ever happens, if my life withstands
the draining force of being misunderstood
time and time again. And because he's good
and honest, and because what's right

maps so well upon the angles of his most intimate wishes
I mourn for him now, well before he passes,
wishing to be for him another walking stick,
dispatching prayers in the only language rich
enough to transcend the way things are:

an old man and his son, fighting a war
in a warzone we all must visit.

Epilogue

Travel Plans

Marbella, Spain

I am going it seems where the wind blows,
the gusts of all I've learned, planed and hollowed
to the shape of a finger, the shape of a finger without
its telltale print. I am going to a place without a name
to my credit, and when I get there, I presume,
there'll be no reward, waiting, for the dolls of my quick wits.
There will be only the ghost of my signature,
a squiggle in wraith-grey, a seal I never wished-for, a slur.

And all my plans to have got to a better place
will prove as nothing, the high tablet of my hopes, razed
before a second line of print, a conquering line I never
planned-for, penned. Let the people about me know
I did my best, my utmost, to travel to the better place,
as they did theirs – but that in the end I had to land at this, and nowhere.

The Escape Of The Prisoner From His Dilemma

Beirut

I cannot read minds.
Each ghost of the other's thoughts passes me by,
formed by the cage of itself.
Each of us thinks in his own private cell
and I don't wish to enter there,

where each one of us lives, barred and scored
by his own small hell – danced by the music of the stars
that guides each, as each tells his own daft tale.

I cannot read minds, and I really don't know
the wherefores behind the waylaid words
I hear at times. The motives of the other are like surds
to me, heights I gape-at, a dilettante, dithering from below.
I cannot read minds and nor

will I ever wish to.

Afterword

The Tribe and The Alabaster City

I started my poetic career in 2006. I had just resigned from a PhD I was (supposedly) working on at Cambridge, under the supervision of Professor Stefan Collini. I recall our last meeting together, bidding each other farewell. Professor Collini was somewhat surprised, but more pressingly perhaps, seemed to be slightly titillated by my decision to resign and to pursue a vocation for writing verse. And I suppose for a scholar like that – one whose body of work has been among many, many other things, poetic in the sense that so much of its brilliance and subsequent success has been the effect of his literary ear for the implicit meanings rendered by voice and tone and attitude (making him one of our leading intellectual historians) – it *would* seem amusing that a young man like myself would make such an about-turn. He did say though, by way of parting advice, that finding a true voice took a certain amount of time, implying therefore for me not to expect to succeed in any palpable sense (de facto or de jure, I suppose) for quite a while. That said, I'd my first poems published in *Agenda Online* in the Summer of 2006, followed close-by with poems published in *The Reader Magazine*, a splendid journal based at the University of Liverpool, and then, bizarrely but thankfully, in *Poetry Review*. And since then, I have been, relatively-speaking, successful as a poet.

As a writer of poetry betimes, I am, or have been at least, highly erratic. Another, but only dovetailing, not mapping, way of saying this, is to say that I write too much. Unlike what is I hope my far more rigorous consistency as a writer of prose in whatever format, poetry in my case has often been what, it might be argued, it should not be, a therapeutic place for venting, directly, transitively and without that reflexive element of good writers that allows for good decisions and choices. This has come to mean that it really is one in ten or one in twenty, even, of my efforts that ends up being a piece that has the necessity, integrity and surprise of a genuine poem. And another reason that the vast bulk of my poetic endeavors end up being waste produce, is that I tend to write impulsively, which means I rarely revisit poems after the maximum half-hour work on them. It seems to me that what I am telling myself, implicitly, by this temperamental facet of my poetic career or, better, vocation, is that if it didn't come naturally, spontaneously, it was never there. This may well be untrue, but it is part and parcel of who I am, fortunately or not, as a writer of poems.

It might be an obvious thing to say for readers of this book that I am guided by my ear much of the time, that the sensual materiality of language is one of my prime motives as a writer, motoring through me with its semiotic music. That is true, but I think it's also true, and perhaps most compellingly so, that even if I tend to be highly emotive and lyrical, I am also, I suppose, quite a reflective writer, meaning that thinking-through something, an image, situation or relationship, that very process, is what drives the sensibility behind these poems. Adding these two observations together, mind and body, this would make me in the arithmetic at hand somewhat of a now-classically-considered 'metaphysical' poet. Perhaps. In any case, the long and short of it is that a poem that succeeds and that is perhaps true to myself, its author, is one whose holistic effect renders the moved reader surprised into some new track of thinking, as well. And then, between mind and body, along the seam where they meet, however ineffably, is the soul. And I think I might be right in calling myself as a poet what many I've noted have called me to date: soulful. But from another angle of vision, the place where mind and body meet is precisely the place where we find instinct, that drive as it were rooted in our bodily and animal natures – which is also the origin at the same time of some of our most sublime creations as human animals.

So. To sum it up in a nice nutshell (between kernel and husk), and being only *slightly* tongue-in-cheek, my poetry is where the tribal dance of who I am meets the alabaster city of whom I'd like to be.

www.ingramcontent.com/pod-product-compliance
Lightning Source LLC
Chambersburg PA
CBHW071356090426
42738CB00012B/3137

* 9 7 8 1 9 9 8 3 0 9 3 3 7 *